Original title:
Wisteria Whispers

Copyright © 2025 Creative Arts Management OÜ
All rights reserved.

Author: Aidan Marlowe
ISBN HARDBACK: 978-1-80566-653-0
ISBN PAPERBACK: 978-1-80566-938-8

Glimpses of Grace in Broken Light

In gardens where the colors clash,
A bee flies by, with quite a dash.
It polls the blooms, then takes a nap,
Dreaming of nectar in a sunny clap.

A squirrel slips, a raccoon stares,
Both pondering life under leafy flares.
The breeze joins in with playful might,
Catching petals on a flighty night.

Vestiges of Time in Petal Form

Petals fall like aged confetti,
As my cat thinks he's a real spaghetti.
Chasing shadows, in a floppy stance,
Turns life's garden into a dance!

A snail makes haste, or so it seems,
While bees compete in buzzing dreams.
The fun of life beneath the leaves,
Is laughter caught in falling sheaves.

The Rhapsody Beneath the Vine

The grapevine sings a silly tune,
While mice cavort beneath the moon.
A cricket strums a plastic string,
Declaring vines the silliest thing!

Two frogs croak verses, out of sync,
Life's an opera when you blink.
In this green world, the jokes align,
With laughter flowing like sweet wine.

Tidal Rhythms of Blooming Vines

As blooms sway with the evening tide,
A hedgehog rolls, no sense of pride.
He trundles forth, unbothered, spry,
In his hedgy world, he'll never fly!

A slip of a leaf, a tumble of fun,
Nature's antics for everyone.
With every giggle, each twist entwined,
Life's a comedy, well-designed.

Inflorescence Impressions

In the garden of giggles, where blooms wear a grin,
Petals tell secrets, of mischief and sin.
The bees buzz in laughter, their dance quite a show,
While butterflies gossip, with gossip to blow.

Colors collide, like a party gone wild,
With daisies in tutus, and roses so styled.
Each blossom's a clown, with their petals all bright,
Under the sun's gaze, it's a carnival light.

The Secret Language of Vines

Those vines twist and turn, like dancers on air,
They whisper sweet nothings, without a care.
A frond gives a nod, while leaves play charades,
   Creating a ruckus, in leafy parades.

Oh, the antics of roots, in their underground game,
They tickle the soil, all vying for fame.
With tendrils all tangled, they plot and they scheme,
In the shade of the shrubs, they giggle and beam.

Silken Sighs in Bloom

In gardens of laughter, where petals will sway,
The flowers throw parties, in their own quirky way.
Their silken attire, a sight to concede,
Dresses made from sunshine, oh, what a breed!

With giggles of petals, and sighs made of dew,
They share all their stories, both old and anew.
A dandelion whispers, 'I'm fluff, not a foe!'
While the lilacs are laughing, just putting on a show.

Beneath the Cascade of Blossoms

Under a cascade, of colors so bright,
The flowers convene, in the warm morning light.
Chortles and chuckles, from petals so fine,
They spin tales of pollen, like they're sipping wine.

With a gander at petals, a chatter so sweet,
A daffodil jokes, 'Hey, this ground's quite a treat!'
While tulips engage in a floral ballet,
They sway to the rhythm, in their own funny way.

Crystalline Spirit Beneath the Arbour

Under the vine, a gnome sits tight,
With tales of mischief, day and night.
He claims the blooms are his great kin,
And steals their scents with a goofy grin.

But flowers giggle, sprinkling cheer,
As they dance mockingly, drawing near.
"Oh, silly sprite, you won't deceive,
These petals know, we won't believe!"

Chronicles of the Twilight Flora

In the dusk, flowers start to plot,
A heist of nectar, quite the shot!
They gather whispers with a wink,
For bees take notes as they all think.

Petals in arms, plotting away,
Sneaking sweets at the end of the day.
With giggles and squeals, they'll take their chance,
In a swaying, whimsical dance!

Petal Pasts and Future Blossoms

Once I heard a bud declare,
"I've seen it all, oh, do beware!"
A while later, it lost its flair,
As petals ruffled in the air.

With each tale of bloom and bee,
The garden chuckled in jubilee.
"Oh blossoms bright, do make amends,
For every tale the humor lends!"

Fragments of Dreams in Bloom

In a realm where petals dream,
One said, "Life's not what it seems!"
They trade their guffaws in moonlight's gleam,
Sharing whispers of a rusty theme.

A dandelion joined, uninvited,
"I blow with laughter, ignited!"
They puffed up big, teasing the night,
With ticklish sleights, what a sight!

The Song of Swaying Blooms

Flowers dance in springtime's breeze,
Bees wear tiny stripes with ease.
Petals laugh and giggle bright,
While ants march to their own delight.

Sunbeams tickle every leaf,
Spreading joy beyond belief.
Squirrels chatter, plotting schemes,
While daisies spill their silly dreams.

Mysteries Amidst the Foliage

Under stars, the secrets play,
Plants gossip in their own way.
Mice in capes, and frogs that sing,
Plotting mischief in the spring.

Caterpillars scheme and plot,
While ladybugs lose track of spot.
In the thicket, laughter's sound,
Echoes wildly all around.

Whispering Trellises at Dusk

Evening falls, the shadows tease,
Adventures brought by laughing trees.
Tiny fairies flit and glide,
Chasing moonlight far and wide.

Crickets share their nightly tales,
Of sleepy heads and silly trails.
With every chirp, a joke they spin,
In the garden, let the fun begin!

Tales from the Garden's Heart

In the patch where veggies thrive,
Radishes and carrots jive.
Tomatoes roll in laughter bright,
As beet greens tango through the night.

Chickens chuckle, feathers ruffled,
In the coop, their giggles muffled.
Turnips gossip, life's a game,
In the garden, none feel the same.

Dappled Light in the Garden

In the garden where the shadows play,
The flowers gossip in a cheeky way.
Bees wear tiny hats and dance around,
While butterflies are making silly sounds.

The sun peeks through, a golden ray,
Tickling petals, come out to sway.
A squirrel drops acorns from on high,
He aims at birds who just squawk and fly.

Threads of Nature's Lullabies

A breeze tells jokes with a rustling laugh,
While daffodils giggle as they take a bath.
Clouds wearing pajamas float by with ease,
The grass joins in with its ticklish tease.

Ladybugs sport polka-dots so bright,
They form a band, playing tunes of delight.
A frog in a top hat leaps with glee,
Croaking along like it's meant to be.

Soft Sounds Amongst the Leaves

Rustling leaves make whispers and sighs,
Tickling noses with nature's surprise.
A rabbit hops by, in a bowtie so neat,
And giggles are heard in the soft summer heat.

The wind tells tales of a quirky old tree,
Who forgot how to dance but insists it's free.
Raccoons in capes are planning a prank,
While mockingbirds imitate a clumsy crank.

The Elegance of Twirling Vines

Vines twist and twirl like they're at a ball,
Dressed in green gowns, they enchant us all.
A caterpillar waltzes, missing a beat,
While grasshoppers tap, trying to be neat.

In this garden's circus, laughter reigns,
With juggling pumpkins and dancing canes.
Even the roses wear sparkling pouts,
As the tomato plants break into shouts!

Echoes of Enchantment

In the garden, giggles bloom,
A squirrel stole my last vacuum.
He dances round with a nutty flair,
While I chase shadows, pulling my hair.

Fairies are plotting cheese-filled schemes,
In gossipy circles, they burst my dreams.
I swear they borrowed my shiny shoes,
Now they prance about in purple hues.

The sun peeks out, a clown in disguise,
Tickling petals that dance and rise.
I trip on vines with a theatrical fall,
Laughing at blooms who saw it all.

So let us toast to the humor in flight,
Where laughs bloom bright in the violet light.
With giggles and chuckles, we'll sing our part,
In a garden of chaos, we'll share our heart.

Beneath the Cascade of Violet

Under drapes of purple delight,
A snail once declared it's a race, not a flight.
While bees held meetings on daisies' heads,
I slipped on petals and awkwardly spread.

The mist in the air is giggling near,
"Did you hear that? They said it's a deer!"
But out pops a rabbit with big floppy ears,
Laughing so hard, he forgot all his fears.

A butterfly fumbled, what a sight to see,
Flying backward, 'Oops, not for me!'
The flowers all chuckle, they know how it goes,
In the land where laughter eternally grows.

So let's dance under this floral spree,
In a game of pranks, just you and me.
With petals as pillows and giggles galore,
We'll spin through the chaos, forever explore.

Lavender Lullabies

In fields of lavender, humor sprouts,
With each gentle breeze, the flowers pout.
A bee with a bowtie, busy and bright,
Accidentally bumped into a kite.

Chasing giggles, the sunlight beams,
While ants conspire with silly dreams.
They write little notes on the grass from above,
As worms roll their eyes at the butterflies' love.

A ladybug lost in a dance so bold,
Mistakes a pancake for a lovely mold.
And the wind chuckles, spreading the jest,
As all of nature joins in the fest.

So sing out loud, among petals so sweet,
Where laughter tickles each tiny beat.
Let's twirl under stars that wink with glee,
In lavender fields, just you and me.

Veils of Violet Dreams

In the twilight where giggles arise,
A hedgehog wearing a hat decides.
With a twirl and a grin, he rolls away,
While all the flowers join in the play.

The moon is laughing, a bright silver ball,
With fairies that prance and tease us all.
A cat in pajamas struts down the lane,
Getting caught in a snare of soft purple grain.

The stars join the fun, they wink and shine,
Creating shadows that twist and twine.
In this dreamy realm, where all can forget,
Laughter flows freely, no rules to set.

So let's chase the night, no reason to hide,
With violet dreams, the world's on our side.
We'll dance through the chaos, with humor supreme,
In a garden alive with whimsical dream.

Gardened Secrets from the Past

In the garden, secrets lie,
The gnomes all giggle on the sly.
Planting tales of wild regret,
What did they sow? We can't forget.

A squirrel with mischief in his eye,
Steals the last of grandma's pie.
The flowers bloom with gossip sweet,
Spilling beans on every seat.

Interwoven Stories of Blossoms

A rose once dated a tulip bright,
They argued over who's more right.
The daisies laughed, they were quite bold,
As tales of love and drama unfold.

Violets started a flower trend,
Who knew that blossoms could offend?
Their petals flapped like whispers tight,
In the daylight, oh what a sight!

An Elegance of Enchanted Blooms

A lily wore a fancy hat,
While talking to a curious cat.
They debated on the best perfume,
But ended up lost in the gloom.

Petunias danced in swaying rows,
Making fun of the downturned clothes.
With every twirl, they let out screams,
In a world where nothing's as it seems.

Symphony of the Tranquil Grove

In the grove, the pine trees sway,
Whispering jokes about the day.
The oak plays bass, with roots that groove,
While willows giggle and sway to move.

Crickets serenade the night,
They brag about their singing flight.
Even the moon can't help but chuckle,
At nature's playful, endless shuffle.

Moonlight Beneath the Canopy

Under the stars, we dance so spry,
Tripping on roots, we laugh and sigh.
A squirrel joins in, with acorn flair,
Who knew woodlands held such debonair?

A moth in a tux, how dapper he seems,
He flutters and twirls, disrupting our dreams.
With grace, he collides into a twig,
From now on, our dance card's quite big!

A raccoon sneaks snacks, with stealthy delight,
Until we catch him—oh what a sight!
He blushes with shame, or so I presume,
And runs off to plot his biscuit-tasting zoom!

The moon shakes her head, amused by the scene,
Nature's soirée with a touch of the keen.
As laughter erupts, under night's gentle reign,
Tomorrow we'll waddle through laughter again!

Serenity in the Arbor's Embrace

Beneath leafy boughs, we sit with glee,
Chasing down dreams like a buzzing bee.
Chatting with crickets, our secret folks,
Sharing snickers with playful stokes.

An owl gives a hoot, like he's pulling our leg,
With eyes wide as saucers, he might just beg.
Shh, don't wake him! He's got a long night,
Plotting and scheming in the fading light.

The breeze joins the laughter, rustling the leaves,
Whispering tales of playful thieves.
A squirrel in shades, sunglasses so bold,
Steals our snacks while we're busy and sold!

With giggles aplenty, and moonlit cheer,
We clink our juice boxes, best friends here.
The trees echo joy, as the evening grows old,
The funniest stories will never grow cold!

Veiled Conversations in Bloom

Petals converse in a giggly hush,
Flirting with bees in a soft golden rush.
"Did you see that?" a daisy exclaimed,
"Oh my, how clumsy!" another one blamed.

Whispers of flowers, secrets to share,
Each with their gossip, a floral affair.
A tulip trips over a rogue weed vine,
"Oops!" she declares, "Next time I'll twine!"

The lilies snicker, swaying with flair,
"Who knew garden gossip could snag such a pair?"
Cacti roll eyes, "We're sharp but discreet,
While you bloom and bluster, we're still kinda neat."

As petals unravel their silly delights,
The sun sets on us, painting the nights.
With laughter suspended in blossoms anew,
We'll bloom with each other, just me and you!

Cascading Azure Sentiments

In fields of blue, we twirl with the breeze,
Chasing our dreams with both giggles and ease.
A butterfly swoops, all grace with a spin,
Crashing right down on my unsuspecting chin!

"Oh dear!" I exclaim, where did you learn?
"To land, I mean flop, it's all in the turn!"
With arms wide open, I catch the next flight,
Only to tumble, a star of the night!

The daisies all cheer; they're my number one fans,
With petals aflutter, and happy plant plans.
A snail shows up, his timing so slow,
He shrugs and just grins, "That's how we roll, yo!"

Clouds giggle softly, they're dancing on high,
As colors descend through the vast evening sky.
With laughter cascading like dew in the morn,
We create magic, 'til the new day is born!

Dance of Delicate Tendrils

The vines entwine with playful glee,
They twist and twirl, oh can't you see?
A tango here, a cha-cha there,
With leafy limbs that wave in air.

The petals giggle, a sight to behold,
In colors bold, their tales unfold.
They jive with joy, dip low to please,
As butterflies join in with ease.

Watch out 'neath the hanging blooms,
Frequent visits cause minor booms.
A clumsy bee trips on a vine,
Ends up buzzing, "Hey, I'm fine!"

Each day they laugh, a wild parade,
In nature's dance, no plans are made.
From dawn till dusk, the fun's alive,
In this ruffled realm, we thrive!

Roots of Serenity

Beneath the earth, those roots conspire,
To giggle and plot, their one desire.
They whisper secrets to the ground,
While tickling worms with laughs profound.

In the soil, they wiggle and squirm,
Creating chaos, a funny term.
"Who needs a dance when we can wiggle?"
A turf war ends up a playful giggle.

"If only the grass could join our shindig,
We'd start a party, oh so big!"
A little ant chimes in, quite keen,
"This rooty affair is the best I've seen!"

So here they plot, in a silent riot,
To make the mundane life a quiet diet.
Their humor flows, deep in their core,
Roots of serenity forevermore!

Lush Reveries Underneath

In shadows deep, where dreams take flight,
The cozy critters dance at night.
A fluffy mouse dons a tiny crown,
While crickets play their whimsical sound.

Frogs leap in synchronized style,
With leaps so grand, they make us smile.
"Who knew the night held such delight?"
Squeaked owl giggles, "Let's dance till light!"

Underneath the lush green drapes,
Chasing each other in funny shapes.
A worm slips in, catches a ride,
On a beetle's back, they laugh and glide.

These secret shenanigans run deep,
Through tangled roots, their fun they keep.
A mirthful band in leafy retreat,
Where the wild emotions can't be beat!

Petal Kisses in the Breeze

In the soft breeze, petals blow,
Kissing cheeks with every show.
They flirt and twirl, like silly sprites,
Dancing softly on sunlit bites.

The flowers giggle, what a tease!
Rustling leaves in a jovial breeze.
"Oh, don't you dare let go of me!"
A daisy yells, quite merrily.

With every gust, a waltz ensues,
Petals spin in vibrant hues.
They swirl around in playful chase,
Painting laughter on every face.

In this bloom brigade up high,
They make the air a soothing sigh.
Each kiss a promise, light and free,
In nature's charm, come dance with me!

Dance of the Amethyst Shadows

In the twilight's silly chuckle,
Shadows prance and sway,
Tiptoeing on their tippy toes,
In a laughter-filled ballet.

Jesters in a purple hue,
Swinging from the vines,
Twisting their mischief well,
In the sunshine that shines.

Around the garden glee ensues,
With every tiny twist,
Even the flowers grin widely,
Valleys of joy persist.

And when the moon starts to giggle,
Stars join in the fun,
The fuchsia blooms all shimmer,
As the night has just begun.

Garden of Lingering Echoes

In a garden where laughter grows,
Echoes play hide and seek,
Ticklish petals burst with joy,
While the bees start to sneak.

A squirrel tells a joke to a twig,
The daisies roll their eyes,
The wind winks at all the trees,
As the sun begins to rise.

Whimsical whispers drift through air,
As flowers share their dreams,
The snickers of the bumblebees,
Float like floating streams.

Among the sweet, fragrant chaos,
Life dances with delight,
Round and round in giggling sound,
'Til the stars greet the night.

Elegies of the Faded Blooms

In a world where petals burst,
With tales of love and glee,
Each faded bloom has a secret,
That giggles just like me.

They whisper of their playful past,
When colors bright did sway,
Now they chuckle all the time,
As if to say, 'Okay!'

Droopy heads can't hide their laughs,
In the afternoon's warm glow,
As butterflies sit back and jest,
With jokes only they know.

And as the sun begins to fade,
They sing their silly tune,
With laughter dancing in the leaves,
They serenade the moon.

A Melody Amongst the Tendrils

Amidst the vines, a melody,
Strums the heart's delight,
Tunes of the jolly little bugs,
Dancing in the night.

Twisting tendrils reach and grab,
Each one with a tune,
While the giggling branches sway,
Underneath the moon.

The lanterns sway like happy feet,
With shadows jumping by,
As blossoms hum their silly songs,
To the winking sky.

A chorus of the zany winds,
Tickles every soul,
In this playful harbor fair,
Where laughter takes its toll.

Threads of Time in Full Bloom

Once I caught a shadow's dance,
It twirled away in a silly prance.
Laughing leaves in playful glee,
   Tickled by the buzzing bee.

Time skips like a child at play,
In nature's game, we lose our way.
I tripped on roots while chasing fate,
A twisted path, oh what a state!

Breezes whisper silly tales,
Of mismatched socks and fancy snails.
The sun chuckles, oh so bright,
As shadows frolic in the light.

So let us weave a merry thread,
In blossoms where the laughter spread.
   For in this garden, joy's the key,
To spin our tales with glee and spree.

A Symphony of Twisting Branches

The branches sway with such a tune,
As squirrels dance beneath the moon.
A symphony of giggles high,
Composed of ants that march on by.

Tap your toes on mossy ground,
A beat of pranks is all around.
Twisting vines in playful fights,
As butterflies wear silly tights.

The wind plays tricks with my hat,
While rabbits join the merry chat.
A symphony of leaves that laugh,
Nature's orchestra, what a gaffe!

With every step, a funny slip,
The branches giggle, what a trip!
In this wild concert, join the tune,
As we twirl 'neath the playful moon.

Secrets in the Sylvan Glow

Underneath the glowing trees,
A secret's there that makes one wheeze.
The flowers gossip, petals shake,
About a frog who danced by a lake.

Whispers float on breezy nights,
A world of mischief, silly sights.
The owls chuckle from their shelf,
As crickets serenade themselves.

I found a snail who paints the town,
In colors bright, oh what a frown!
For every splash, he slips and sloshes,
In a tale where awkwardness posh-es!

So come along and take a look,
At secrets growing like a book.
In this glade where laughter's the glow,
You'll find the fun that makes you go!

Blooming Under the Silvery Moon

At night beneath the silver light,
The flowers giggle, what a sight!
They bloom in hues of silly dreams,
As fireflies dance in playful schemes.

A cat with glasses reads a book,
While dreaming of a cozy nook.
The petals chuckle, twirling round,
To music made without a sound.

In moonlit gardens, nothing's plain,
As rabbits juggle rain and grain.
With every hop, mischief's afoot,
The night is young and full of loot!

So let us bloom in laughter's light,
And spin our tales till morning bright.
For under moons with giggles grown,
We find the joy, the fun we've sown.

Luminous Tapestries of Twilight

In twilight's glow, the vines conspire,
A laugh erupts, a gentle fire.
Beneath the blooms, the squirrels dance,
As shadows twirl, they take their chance.

The flowers giggle, bright and bold,
With little stories yet untold.
They swing from branches, just a tease,
Come join the fun, if you please!

With scents that tickle, oh so sweet,
A fragrant joy can't be discreet.
The butterflies, they wear a grin,
As petals laugh and play within.

So let the vines wrap round your heart,
In this grand garden, play your part.
With twinkling stars and chuckles near,
It's twilight's laughter, loud and clear.

Shadows of Serene Blooms

Amidst the leaves, a chortle floats,
A shadowy giggle, playful moats.
The blooms conspire in leafy shade,
As petals rustle, plans are laid.

The bees buzz by, with jokes to share,
While dandelions flip their hair.
They whisper secrets, soft and sly,
As butterflies burst forth to fly.

A frog in green starts to croak,
With punchlines sharper than a poke.
He leaps and bounds, the crowd's delight,
With every hop, he steals the night.

In leafy shadows, laughter soars,
A garden party, who needs doors?
With every bloom, a comedic flair,
In nature's jest, we lose all care.

Songs of the Lush Canopy

In the canopy, a choir sings,
With chirps and hoots, they share their flings.
The raindrops tap a funny beat,
As branches sway and dance their feet.

A squirrel strums on a twig guitar,
While crickets chirp, they raise the bar.
The leaves all sway like silly hats,
As nature giggles with all its chats.

A parrot cracks a joke so bright,
With colors bold, it takes flight.
The wind whispers tales from afar,
In this lush haven, laughter's star.

So gather 'round, let voices rise,
In the green above, hear the surprise.
With smiles and tunes, the day is bright,
In our canopy, all feels just right.

Spun from the Essence of Vines

The vines entwine, a knitted jest,
With every loop, they bring their best.
They twirl and spin, a joyful crew,
As laughter echoes through the dew.

A pip from below, a sweet surprise,
As grapes recount their funny lies.
They roll and bounce, a playful race,
With all the blooms, they find their place.

The tendrils tickle, oh what fun,
A nature's party has begun.
With each new twist, the giggles grow,
In this winding runway, laughter flows.

So join the twist of nature's play,
In woven joy, we'll dance today.
With every vine, a sprightly cheer,
In the garden's heart, we find our sphere.

Petal Pathways Over Time

Once I tripped on petals bright,
Thought I'd dance, but lost my height.
Springs of laughter filled the air,
As I rolled without a care.

Butterflies laughed, did a jig,
Nearby a squirrel tried to dig.
Flowers giggled, petals waved,
In this garden, we misbehaved.

The sun, it peeked 'round the bend,
With mischief, it chose to bend.
Tulips joined in, quite the show,
As I laughed too hard, oh no!

Time, it strolled with a grin,
Found its shoes, forgot the spin.
But in this garden, joy's the rhyme,
We'll dance through these petal pathways of time.

Whispered Promises in Lilac

In lilac blooms, I made a vow,
To sing like birds, but wow, oh wow!
My voice, it squeaked like rubber toys,
While friends all giggled, oh what joys!

Bees kept buzzing 'round my head,
I jumped, and then I tripped, oh dread!
They whispered secrets, very sweet,
While I tried dodging dancing feet.

Laughter floated on the breeze,
As squirrels chuckled in the trees.
A lilac promise on my tongue,
Yet I sang tunes completely wrong!

But in these blooms, we found delight,
With whispered laughter, all felt right.
Life's a song, a silly tune,
Best shared beneath the lilac moon.

Enchanted Treasures of Spring

In springtime's treasure hunt I ran,
With pockets full of bits and ban.
I found a sock, a lost old shoe,
And wondered how they made it too!

The daisies giggled in the sun,
As I searched for a bit of fun.
I dug a hole, oh what a mess,
Uncovered fluff, but not success!

The robin winked as if to say,
"Keep searching, there's a game to play!"
I found a pebble, smooth and round,
And claimed it as my prize profound.

These springtime treasures full of glee,
Bring laughter, happiness, and me.
In every corner, magic's found,
As joyful moments spin around.

Cradled by Clusters of Comfort

In cozy clusters, here we sit,
Amid the blooms, where giggles flit.
The daisies tell the funniest tales,
While butterflies flap with flappy sails.

A bumblebee in fancy dress,
Zooms past my face, oh what a mess!
I ducked, I hid, but lost my hat,
The flowers chimed, "What's up with that?"

With petals soft, we made a throne,
A comfy spot, we claimed as our own.
A jumbled group, but the spirit's right,
In these clusters, joy takes flight.

So here we laugh, embraced by cheer,
In nature's warmth, we shed a tear.
Each petal whispers secrets sweet,
In comfort's cradle, life's a treat.

Tangles of Time and Petals

In the garden, time does twirl,
With blooms that spin and dance and swirl.
A bumblebee in a funny hat,
Sips nectar while doing a little chat.

The sunbeams giggle, tickling toes,
As petals gossip in comical prose.
With every breeze, the whispers tease,
Making the flowers giggle with ease.

The gardener trips on tangled roots,
While finding the funniest of fruits.
A cucumber jokes, 'I'm in a pickle!'
While zucchini rolls with a cheerful chuckle.

In this garden, bright and gay,
Every flower shines in a silly way.
As laughter blooms, the day takes flight,
Turning the mundane into pure delight.

Echoes in the Grape Arbor

In the shade of vines, secrets hide,
Where grapes hang low, and laughter rides.
A plump little grape, round as can be,
Sings about life, oh so carefree.

The laughter of leaves, a rustling sound,
As squirrels debate on the best nuts found.
They argue and prance, not a care in sight,
While shadows play games in the fading light.

A fox wanders by with a wink of an eye,
His tail like a banner, he scampers by.
'What's a fox? A clever old chap,'
'Just here for the grapes and maybe a nap!'

In the grape arbor, fun never ends,
With antics and giggles, the joy ascends.
Every corner holds a story to tell,
Of laughter, of folly, all blossoming well.

Secrets Held in Soft Shades

In the soft shadows where secrets play,
A lazy cat snoozes the day away.
Dreaming of mice that dance on the wall,
While dandelions plot a spring-time ball.

The sun peeks through, with a friendly grin,
As fairies giggle, inviting him in.
They sip on dew drops, with whispers so spry,
Jokingly asking, 'Can you even fly?'

A frog on a lily pads on a quest,
For the juiciest flies, he will jest.
With every leap, he quacks a new rhyme,
Making the pond burst out with chime.

In soft shades, mysteries unfurl,
As flowers sway and young dreams whirl.
With laughter and shade, time takes a break,
In a world where hilarity's never opaque.

A Symphony of Twisted Vines

Among the twisted vines of lore,
A symphony plays, and oh, what a score!
The leaves rustle gently, keeping the beat,
While ants waltz along in their party suite.

A cricket recites a poem so bright,
As daisies peek out, quite the sight!
They sway to the music, a joyful parade,
Bumbling around in their floral charade.

A hedgehog rolls in a ball of delight,
Not quite a dancer, but gives it a bite.
With each wiggle and jiggle, the world spins round,
As merriment thrives, in nature it's found.

In this symphony rich with funny tunes,
Under lavender skies and glowing balloons,
Each note a chuckle, each rest a sigh,
In the garden of giggles, the spirits fly high.

The Poetry of Twirling Tendrils

In a garden where laughter grows,
Tendrils twist in silly flows,
A cat leaps high, caught in a mess,
Chasing shadows, oh what a stress!

The sun peeks through, a wobbly beam,
Dancing vines play peek-a-boo, it seems,
A squirrel throws a nut with flair,
And lands right on my poor friend's hair!

With every breeze, the giggles rise,
Spinning tales of tangled sighs,
Watch the flowers sway and sway,
As bees do the cha-cha all day!

So come and join this twisty spree,
Where nature spins its own decree,
Laughing till our bellies ache,
In this garden of giggles, make no mistake!

Norse Tales Under the Arbour

In shades of purple, tales unfold,
A Viking's helmet, all bright and bold,
He trips on roots, oh what a sight,
As flowers chuckle in pure delight!

The gods up high take note of this,
Thor drops his hammer, can't believe his bliss,
While Loki laughs, shadows he sows,
Making mischief where the breeze blows!

With a shiver of leaves, the stories spin,
Of giants and trolls and the pickle they're in,
They dance and tumble, roots entwined,
Laughter echoing, oh how they'd find!

Under the arbour, the tales arise,
Mixing laughter with zephyr sighs,
Grab your horn, let's feast in glee,
Norse legends live in silly spree!

Glimmers Through Cascading Petals

Petals tumble, a confetti fall,
Spinning through the air, a floral ball,
A dog chases, tail wagging fast,
He jumps and rolls, what a joyous blast!

Sunshine dances, a cheeky glow,
Rabbits hop around on toe,
One slips, lands in a flower bed,
With pollen sticking to his head!

A breeze giggles, tickles the ground,
As daisies sway with a silly sound,
While bumblebees buzz a clever tune,
Frogs join in under the moon!

So let yourself swirl in this floral breeze,
Laughing with nature so eager to please,
Among the petals and joy's bright glow,
Silly moments are where we'll grow!

Surrendering to the Fragrant Dance

In fragrant air, the giggles twirl,
Dancers whirl in a floral swirl,
A chicken clucks to beat the band,
While daisies join, oh isn't it grand!

The flowers sway with a rhythm divine,
To the beat of life, like funky wine,
A bee bumps in, a disco queen,
Laughing at moves that can't be seen!

The garden blooms, laughter breaks free,
As we all join, you and me,
Together we spin, surrender in glee,
In the fragrant dance, wild and free!

So let's embrace every silly chance,
Under the petals, come join the dance,
With every giggle, embrace the trance,
Life's a party, join the romance!

The Language of Amethyst Blooms

In the garden, petals chat,
Gossiping about the cat.
With a laugh, they shake and sway,
Making puns in a floral way.

Bees eavesdrop, with buzzing glee,
Taking notes on floral decree.
A blossom winks, a daisy's grin,
Who said that blooms can't wear a pin?

Sunlight giggles through the leaves,
Tickling stems with light reprieves.
A tulip spins a silly tale,
Of how the daisies set the sail.

Laughing hues in the bright daylight,
Paint the scene with delight in sight.
Amethysts in playful tease,
Craft a language that aims to please.

Drifting on a Breeze of Blooms

Petals drift like a paper plane,
Spreading laughter in the rain.
They dance along the whirling air,
Tickling noses without a care.

A rose tells secrets of the sun,
While violets giggle, oh what fun!
They tease the clouds for getting lost,
In their dance, there's no such cost.

A playful breeze joins in the game,
Whirling around, calling each name.
Dandelions puff with delight,
As pollen sprouts take on flight.

Blossoms chime as the wind does blow,
Swaying gently in a floral show.
With whispers sweet and tales so bright,
Drifting blooms bring pure delight.

Enigmas of the Flora Veil

Underneath the leafy cloak,
Blooms concoct their inside joke.
A lily winks, a petal sighs,
While violets plot in disguise.

What do daisies dare to dream?
Plotting mischief, it would seem.
They giggle softly as they scheme,
Beneath the plants, it's quite the theme.

In the shadows, laughter flows,
Petals gossip, here's how it goes:
A sunflower wobbles with delight,
To spill the beans on blooms at night.

Their chuckles fill the evening air,
While roses brush away their care.
Underneath the stars so bright,
Flora's enigmas take their flight.

A Canopy of Colorful Secrets

Underneath the leafy dome,
Blooms gather 'round—far from home.
With whispers shared in hues so bright,
Secrets spill as they take flight.

Crimson buds burst into laughter,
While lilacs sing their happy chapter.
A canopy alive with cheer,
As petals gossip, lend an ear.

When the wind comes, they shout and sway,
Playing tag throughout the day.
Chasing shades of yellow and green,
In vibrant games rarely seen.

Beneath this canopy of cheer,
Each color finds a voice to hear.
So join the blooms in mirthful play,
Where secrets dance and colors sway.

Glistening Trails of Amethyst

In a garden dripping purple,
Silly bees buzz on a mission.
One swayed too hard, lost its grip,
Now it's stuck in a floral rendition.

Petals dance in the gentle breeze,
Down they tumble, oh what a sight!
A ladybug slides, falls with ease,
Only to bounce back, what a delight!

Beneath a vine that tickles the sky,
A puppy pounces, oh what a mess!
Trying to catch a butterfly,
But lands smack-dab in the floral dress!

With laughter echoing through the blooms,
A party erupts among the stems.
Friends gather beneath nature's rooms,
Who knew flowers could cause such mayhem?

Whispers of the Fading Sun

The sun dips low, throwing shadows wide,
A cat leaps, then crinkles its nose.
Chasing its tail, it forgot to hide,
And now it's caught where the soft grass grows.

Birds chuckle high on the evening wires,
Making up tales of the day gone wrong.
Such antics spark their playful fires,
While crickets join in with their evening song.

The twilight sky begins to pout,
As fireflies dance their silly jig.
Swishing softly, they twist about,
"Catch us if you can!" they laugh and dig.

With giggles swirling amid the dusk,
Every glance is a treasure to find.
Nature's jest is a joy we trust,
In these moments, we leave worries behind.

Tangled in Soft Embrace

Vines curl playfully around the fence,
A squirrel races, all speed and flair.
With paws in their midst, it makes no sense,
Now knotted up, it runs with despair.

A chubby toadstool winks from afar,
Chasing a breeze down its silken slide.
It trips on a root, oh how bizarre,
And lands in a puddle, what a ride!

Under the arch where the sweetness blends,
A rabbit hops in its own little flight.
Noticing trouble, it giggles and bends,
As flowers start dancing, lighting the night.

With laughter ringing through leafy halls,
And secrets hidden deep in the green,
Nature plays tricks and encourages calls,
Celebrating joy in the quirkiest scene.

Beneath a Sky of Lavender

Clouds fluff like cotton, soft and serene,
A toddler runs wild with a dandelion.
Sneezing and giggling, a part in between,
"Look at me fly!" he says, such a lion!

The breeze sings softly to lavender skies,
While bunnies hop in their playful race.
Each twist and tumble, a friendly surprise,
Leaves them all laughing, what a warm place!

A dance in the air from the evening bee,
Who forgot its route, oh what a blunder!
Zipping in circles, "Can't you see me?"
Buzzing away, a comedic wonder!

As twilight blankets the garden tonight,
Every flower wears a giggle-bright grin.
Under this canvas, oh what a sight,
Life is a riot where laughter begins!

Harmonies of Bloom and Shade

In the garden's dance, a bug did prance,
Wearing shades as if at a summer bash.
It stumbled on petals, lost in a trance,
While bees buzzed by, trying not to crash.

A squirrel in a tie, conducting the show,
With acorns as notes, he played quite the tune.
The flowers applauded, putting on a glow,
As butterflies flitted, a colorful boon.

Laughter erupted from plants in the sun,
As they shared tales of a gopher's chase.
The petals giggled, the leaves had their fun,
In the shade of the blooms, they found their place.

When sunlight dips low, the laughter won't cease,
A nightly performance by crickets at play.
The garden, alive with its sweet little peace,
Hums a melody night that dances away.

A Lament for Fallen Flora

Oh, the tragedy struck with a gust of the breeze,
Petals tumbled down like a sad, soggy sock.
A dandelion sighed, 'How can it be,
I was once the belle, now a weed in a block?'

The roses all wept, shedding dew for the show,
'Where have our friends gone, our beauty, our flair?'
While daisies rejoiced, shouting, 'We're the stars,
Let's dance in the wind, for we haven't a care!'

In crowded chaos, a tulip fell flat,
Cried out, 'Help me up, I've got you a joke!'
But the lily just giggled and said, 'That's no mat,
Just embrace the ground; it's a soft, flowery cloak!'

So as petals decay, they laugh through their pain,
In the cycle of bloom, in the soil, they'll lie.
For humor finds roots in a fragile domain,
In the fading of colors, new stories will fly.

Shadows Caught in Blooming Light

In the morning glow, shadows pirouette,
A daffodil grinned, swaying left and right.
While tulips took bets on a plant pet duet,
And sunflowers sighed, basking in their might.

A squirrel in a mask, claiming to be grand,
Styled with a paw on a blossom's sweet face.
The petals just laughed, forming a neat band,
Conducting the chaos with charm and with grace.

With each gust of wind, came a whisper of cheek,
A breeze pulled the geraniums into a spin.
While ferns told tall tales, their antics unique,
In the theater of green, each plant wore a grin.

Even shadows had fun, taking center stage,
As they danced on the ground, in a leafy parade.
Such laughter they found, in a natural cage,
In the blooming light, all worries would fade.

Veils of Color and Calm

Beneath bows of petals, a ruckus ensued,
Every daisy was asking, 'Who wore it best?'
In a cape of chiffon, the pansy just brooded,
While the lilies all laughed, relieved of their jest.

A bumblebee buzzed, completely unaware,
Of the subtle debate on the fashion displayed.
'In stripes or in spots, is it too much to wear?'
Yet it carried their nectar, on mission it stayed.

Around them, the sun tossed confetti of light,
As blooms exchanged gossip, a comic affair.
The violets chimed in, 'Is anyone right?'
While the peonies giggled, planting new flair.

In this carnival of hues, worries were light,
With petals as allies, camaraderie soared.
For in laughter and blooms, hearts felt the delight,
In colors and calm, the world grew adored.

Enchanted Silhouettes at Dusk

In the twilight's playful glow,
The shadows dance, high and low.
A squirrel dons a tiny hat,
Chasing dreams and a rubber cat.

The flowers giggle in the breeze,
Tickled by the buzzing bees.
While fancy frogs wear snazzy ties,
Debating under starry skies.

With whispers swirling in the air,
A rabbit winks without a care.
While owls compete in jest and jive,
These antics keep the night alive.

So join the fun and take a seat,
As nature's charm is quite the treat.
With colors bright and spirits high,
We'll laugh 'til moonbeams wave goodbye.

Whirling in the Garden's Mystery

In a garden where the giggles bloom,
A ladybug zooms past the broom.
She twirls through petals and bright green ferns,
While wormy friends strike silly turns.

The daisies hold a dance-off grand,
As the sun spills over the land.
Each blossom spins with glee and fright,
Fumbling under the midday light.

A butterfly slips on honeydew,
Bumping into the kookie crew.
Together they laugh in the shadiest nooks,
Writing silly songs in their storybooks.

As laughter echoes through the ground,
The roots join in to make a sound.
In this haven where joy takes flight,
The garden thrives with sheer delight.

Fleeting Reflections of Serendipity

In puddles deep where giggles hide,
A frog's leap turns into a glide.
He lands with flair on a sleeping snail,
Who thinks it's merely a funny tale.

The chirping birds make a symphony,
Creating notes of pure cacophony.
With shrieks that mimic a wild parade,
Each note a prank that nature made.

Sunflowers bend in a comical bow,
As if to say, 'We're silly, wow!'
A breeze arrives to join the mime,
While ants juggle crumbs, oh what a crime!

With joy that dances in every leaf,
This whimsical world defies belief.
So chase the giggles, don't let them flee,
In these fleeting moments, you'll find glee.

Beneath the Marie's Canopy

Under a canopy of laughter bright,
Where whispers blend with sheer delight.
A mouse on stilts gives quite a show,
While bunnies laugh as they steal the dough.

The branches sway, tap dancing trees,
Make faces while swaying with ease.
Tiny gnomes in silly hats,
Have tea with squirrels and chitchat.

The shadows play tag on the lush green floor,
As fireflies twinkle, begging for more.
Each wave of joy creates a rhyme,
Tickled pink by the hands of time.

So gather 'round this joyful spree,
Where nature hosts the wildest spree.
Let every giggle brightly soar,
Beneath the Marie's, forevermore.

Cascades of Lavender Light

In gardens where the giggles bloom,
Lavender hangs like perfume.
Bees buzz with silly pride,
While butterflies take a joyride.

The sun peeks through tangled vines,
Tickling the leaves in funny lines.
Flowers wink with brilliant cheer,
Pretending not to hear the deer.

A squirrel dances with a leaf,
A tiny dance of pure mischief.
As petals join the jolly spree,
We laugh at nature's glee.

So let us dance under the sky,
With vibrant dreams that flutter by.
In this world where colors play,
Laughter blooms and joy's our way.

The Veil of Time and Bloom

In circles round the blossoms spin,
A clock just ticked out a silly grin.
The petals blush in playful jest,
Competing grains from nature's best.

"Oh, dear bloom, what's your secret?
Do you giggle when I peek at?
Your petals shimmer like a crown,
Do they laugh while falling down?"

Leaves whisper tales of absent mind,
Of lovers lost and flowers blind.
Yet every joke is a timeless one,
Beneath a sun that's just too fun.

Thus blooms the laughter in the shade,
In every breeze, a jest is made.
Let time pass with a chuckle bright,
In gardens wrapped in soft delight.

In the Company of Petals

Gather 'round, oh friends so sweet,
Let's mingle here where petals meet.
With laughter twirling in the air,
Such jolly blooms are hard to spare.

The daisies play a merry game,
While tulips giggle, oh, the fame!
Forget me nots whisper sly jokes,
As clovers chuckle with their folks.

We chat in colors, bright and bold,
Sharing secrets that never grow old.
A flower's tale, a weed's wild laugh,
Nature's comedy, our happy craft.

So come, dear friends, let's cheer aloud,
In this garden, let's feel proud.
Where petals dance and spirits lift,
Laughter's the sweetest gift.

Enchanted Arbor of Solitude

Oh, what a sight, the boughs so grand,
In solitude, let's make our stand.
With petals pink and leaves in play,
Each rustling breeze has much to say.

The shadows tease, and giggles swirl,
In this enchanted, swirling twirl.
A brook nearby hums a light tune,
As if it knows the sun and moon.

Here solitude wears a feathered hat,
While nature laughs at this and that.
Every twig has a story to tell,
In this quirky, leafy cell.

So let's recline beneath the trees,
On fragrant cushions of gentle breeze.
In this arbor, we laugh and sigh,
Finding joy as the moments fly.

Lacing Dreams with Lavender

In gardens where the snails convene,
They talk of dreams, both odd and keen.
A mouse in a hat, a frog with flair,
Claiming they're the best dressers there.

With flowers strung as necklaces bright,
They dance under stars, oh what a sight!
A bee's got rhythm, a worm can groove,
As laughter bubbles, they all approve.

The wind giggles, whispering tunes,
While crickets join in with humorous croons.
Each petal tosses jokes in the air,
While dandelions tease without a care.

In slumber's embrace, silliness stays,
Beneath the lavender's fragrant haze.
An oddball crew, together they scheme,
Lacing their night with laughter and dream.

Charmed Conversations with Nature

In the heart of the fabled wood,
The trees gossip like they really should.
Squirrels debate the best acorn stash,
While owls roll their eyes at the latest bash.

Butterflies tease with their fluttery flight,
As ants form a line, oh what a sight!
A rabbit shouts, 'I'm the king of the hill!'
While hedgehogs chime in, 'Let's have a thrill!'

The flowers nod, sharing jokes in bloom,
While grasshoppers plot to dance in the gloom.
Laughter echoes through every green nook,
As frogs take a plunge in a nearby brook.

With every whisper, joy takes its form,
As nature's charm becomes the norm.
In a world of whimsy and playful cheer,
The banter of blooms fills the atmosphere.

Ethereal Embrace of the Grove

In the grove where giggles sprout,
Even the shadows begin to shout.
A tree has a pun, oh what a clown,
While flowers exchange their gossip in brown.

Breezes tease the branches high,
As clouds drift lazily, wondering why.
'You look like cotton candy!' says a leaf,
With a chuckle that causes nature's relief.

Fireflies twinkle, winking with glee,
In search of the best joke to decree.
A squirrel jests about his nutty plight,
As the moon rolls its eyes, shining so bright.

In laughter's embrace, the night flies fast,
Weaving together the present and past.
A grove filled with humor, nature's delight,
Where whimsy dances under the moonlight.

Odors of Evening's Embrace

As the sun dips low with a wink and a sigh,
The scents of the evening hum softly by.
Lavender chuckles and roses debate,
While daisies giggle, "We're all first-rate!"

In the twilight glow, mischief unfolds,
With a carpet of laughter in hues of gold.
A cabbage craves glory, a peony's flair,
While petunias just tweet their poetry in air.

The evening unrolls like a whimsical scroll,
Where scents mingle freely, igniting the soul.
A candle's aroma offers a tease,
Inviting all cats to scratch at the leaves.

Under the cloak of mysterious night,
The world fills with giggles and aromatic light.
With every sweet whiff, the joy starts to climb,
In a rhapsody fragrant, transcending all time.

A Dance of Twilight Secrets

In twilight's glow, we twirl and spin,
A dance of secrets, let the fun begin.
With vines that giggle, and leaves that sway,
We toss our worries, come what may.

The moonlight chuckles, the stars do cheer,
As blossoms tumble, with no hint of fear.
A squirrel joins in, with acorn hats,
Together we waltz, like silly brats.

Laughter lingers, under boughs we weave,
In every twist, a moment to believe.
With each soft rustle, a friendly jest,
Nature's rhythm, we dance with zest.

As shadows stretch, the night takes flight,
We shimmy and shake, till dawn's first light.
With petals fluttering, a cheerful sight,
In this midnight ball, we're all delight.

The Joy of Blossoms Whispered

Upon the breeze, sweet giggles waltz,
Blossoms chant tales about their faults.
A rose pipes up, with petals so neat,
"I tried to bloom like a sunflower, sweet!"

The daisies snicker, as they share their dreams,
"Who knew we'd sprout with such hype, it seems?"
"Fame can be fickle," a tulip declares,
"Just look at my neighbor; no one compares!"

With petals brushing, they trade hearty laughs,
While bees buzz by, with their silly gaffs.
"Join us for tea, you garden mate,
We'll sip and share till it's far too late!"

As sunlight fades, the laughter will grow,
In this secret garden, there's always a show.
With humor in petals and secrets in bloom,
A tapestry woven, dispelling the gloom.

The Whispering Garden's Lament

The garden sighs, with secrets it keeps,
Underneath rocks where the old toad leaps.
"Did you hear that?" the daisies cry,
A rumor's afloat, let's give it a try!

They whisper of gnomes with misplaced socks,
And squirrels that hold wild acorn talks.
A tulip snickers, "I saw it today,
He wore a twinkle on his brow in play!"

With howls of laughter from vine-covered walls,
They chuckle and tumble, avoiding the falls.
"Oh dear, not again!" a pansy screams wide,
As petals catch giggles that leap and slide.

In shadows unseen, a joke takes flight,
Amongst the green whispers of pure delight.
Though wrinkles and woes may hang in the air,
The garden sings on, nothing can compare.

Journals of the Swaying Vines

A vine in the corner, with stories to tell,
Of fumbles and tumbles, it knows them all well.
"It's all in the sway," it remarks with a wink,
"Here's a page from my book, come, take a peek!"

With ink made from nectar, the tales flow on free,
Of critters that dance, oh, what a sight to see!
"Last week," it mentions, "I witnessed a show,
Where a snail took the stage, and a worm stole the glow!"

In the quiet of shadows, the vines softly jest,
As day turns to twilight, they plot their next quest.
"Let's create mayhem, what a grand plan,
I'll roll down the fence, catch me if you can!"

With each gentle sway, a secret's revealed,
Of laughter and giggles, no worries concealed.
In journals of joy, the vines spin their yarn,
Creating a garden, both lively and warm.

Lilac Hues of Twilight

In twilight's glow, the blooms all dance,
Their lilac hues, a floral romance.
A bee on a mission, buzzed with delight,
Crashing petals, oh what a sight!

The squirrels conspire, with nuts in tow,
Performing their acrobatics, putting on a show.
While butterflies giggle, flitting about,
Hatching plans that leave us in doubt!

A garden gnome grins with a cheeky joke,
As rainclouds gather, threatening to soak.
With all this fun, who needs a plan?
Nature's got laughter; come join the clan!

When twilight fades, the stars pop out,
Vines still whisper, still full of clout.
So grab a drink, and raise a cheer,
To lilac hues, let's spread the gear!

Secrets Beneath the Vines

Beneath the vines, there lie some tales,
Of sneaky cats and adventurous snails.
Laughter erupts from hidden nooks,
As ducks wear hats and read their books!

The garden laughs as the sun goes down,
A hedgehog chef, wearing a crown.
He stirs up soup from raindrops and dew,
While ladybugs sing a merry tune too!

The moon peeks in with a twinkling grin,
Catching the rabbits as they begin.
They hop and twirl, throwing flowers high,
Who knew a garden could be so spry?

With secrets kept by the leaves so green,
Each day reveals a silly scene.
A world of wonder, where chuckles align,
Underneath the curious vines, we dine!

Echoes in the Garden

In the garden's heart, echoes resound,
Laughter and chatter swirl all around.
A parakeet croaks a comedic song,
While daisies nod, joining along!

A flower pot slipped from the gate,
Rolling like thunder—it's running late!
The cats play soccer, their tails in flight,
Chasing around till the fall of night.

The sunflowers giggle, so tall and grand,
As watermelon slices make a stand.
They throw a feast beneath the stars,
With fruit and snacks from Mars to Tars!

As echoes linger, the night grows wild,
Every bug and beast a playful child.
Together we laugh till we hit the hay,
In this garden realm, we live and play!

Surrender to the Scent

When scents collide, we lose control,
A skip in our step, oh what a stroll!
Who knew that roses could tickle our nose,
While minty breath of a fox still glows?

The lavender tickles with fragrance so sweet,
As fireflies dance around our feet.
A cocktail of aromas, a funny affair,
Like skunks in tuxedos—would you dare?

Flavors entwine with each gentle breeze,
Causing giggles among the trees.
Grapes roam free on their jellybean quest,
As tulips wear hats, oh what a jest!

So surrender to scents that tickle the air,
The garden will guide you to laughter and care.
With colors and fragrances wild and free,
Join in the fun, come play with me!

Where Dreams Cling to Branches

In the garden where socks seem to roam,
Dreams drape lightly on branches of foam.
Squirrels debate if it's too hot to play,
While the birds laugh at their feathered ballet.

A raccoon recites, with a serious face,
His philosophy on the art of slow pace.
Blossoms chuckle as they wiggle and sway,
While bees breakdance; they just can't delay.

Clouds float by in a curious glance,
Giggling softly at the flowers' dance.
The breeze joins in with a tickle and tease,
Nature's own duo, a pair full of ease.

So here we stand, in laughter's embrace,
Sharing a joke that time cannot chase.
With dreams that cling like sweet sugared dew,
The garden bursts forth, all giggles and hue.

Murmurs of the Blossom

Petals gossip like old friends in the shade,
Trade silly secrets on how blooms are made.
A butterfly flutters with tales to unfold,
Of flowers who dared to be daringly bold.

They tease the old willow for being too slow,
While the daisies plan to put on a show.
A critter with glasses suggests a grand play,
With roles filled by roots, come join the array!

With whispers of humor that float on the air,
Violet giggles and pinks of despair.
The sun shares a wink as it shines from above,
While sprouting laughter, the garden sings love.

The world spins and twirls in a fanciful way,
As blossoms and breezes share joy for the day.
So listen closely, let the mirth resonate,
In the cradle of petals, pure magic awaits.

Tranquil Shades of Spring

Beneath the green leaves, where shadows play,
Laughter erupts in a light-hearted fray.
A ladybug jokes about size and her luck,
As she struts her stuff, feeling terribly pluck.

Caterpillars argue about who's the best,
While crickets chirp, "We'll put you to the test!"
Nature's own sunshine spills warmth on the floor,
As flowers join in for a waltzing encore.

The breeze carries whispers of giggles and cheer,
A chorus of petals, their sound crystal clear.
The trees crack a grin at the follies below,
Where springtime delights in a delightful show.

The sun takes a bow, the day softly fades,
While the garden hums quiet jokes that it made.
In tranquil shades where laughter takes spring,
Feel the joy that the season will bring.

Beneath A Canopy of Dreams

Underneath branches, the laughter flows free,
Breezes carry secrets from flower to bee.
A frog croaks a joke that's beyond its own kin,
While dragonflies tease, "We'll just swoop in!"

Squirrels debate shade in a comedic plight,
As shadows dance lightly, a humorous sight.
The sun bursts through, with a grin wide and bright,
Casting silver linings in playful delight.

Jasmine swaps stories with daisies so neat,
Of crushes they've had, oh, what a sweet treat!
A plant gives a wink, like a cheeky old friend,
Under this canopy, laughter won't end.

In the realm of petals, where joy visits dreams,
A symphony of chuckles flows in cheerful streams.
So join in the mirth beneath nature's gleam,
With abundant laughter, let your spirit beam.

www.ingramcontent.com/pod-product-compliance
Lightning Source LLC
Chambersburg PA
CBHW072147200426
43209CB00051B/828